Our World

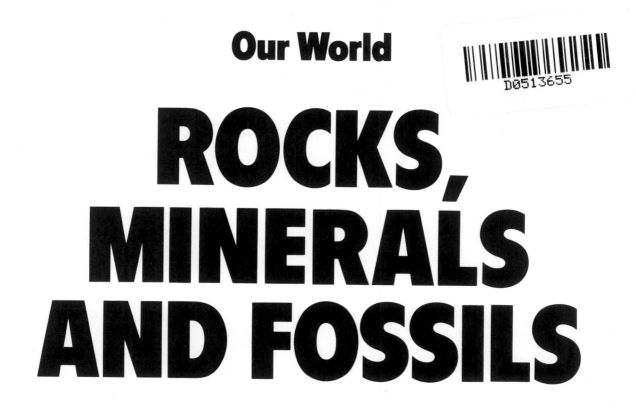

ROCKS, MINERALS AND FOSSILS

Keith Lye

Wayland

Titles in this series

Coasts

Deserts

The Earth in Space

Grasslands

Jungles and Rainforests

Mountains

Polar Regions

Pollution and Conservation

Rivers and Lakes

Rocks, Minerals and Fossils

Seas and Oceans

Temperate Forests

Volcanoes and Earthquakes

Weather and Climate

First published in 1988 by
Wayland (Publishers) Ltd
61 Western Road, Hove
East Sussex BN3 1JD, England

Edited by Jollands Editions
Series design by Malcolm Smythe
Book design by Malcolm Walker

British Library Cataloguing in Publication Data
Lye, Keith
 Rocks, minerals and fossils
 1. Fossils. 2. Geology
 I. Title   II. Walker, Malcolm   III. Series
 560

  ISBN 1–85210–607–7

Typeset by DP Press, Sevenoaks, Kent
Printed in Italy by G. Canale & C.S.p.A., Turin
Bound in Belgium by Casterman S.A.

Front cover, main picture Vixen Tor, a granite outcrop on Dartmoor, England.

Front cover, inset Amethyst crystal.

Back cover, inset Fossil fish from the Devonian period.

Contents

Inside the earth

The earth is one of the nine planets in the solar system. Four planets — Jupiter, Saturn, Uranus and Neptune — are huge, low-density balls of gas. The others, including earth, are dense, rocky bodies.

Several theories have been proposed to explain the formation of the solar system. Most scientists now think that it originated as a vast rotating disc of gas and dust, fragments of exploded stars. Material was drawn towards the centre of the disc to form a dense mass, which became a new star, the sun. The planets, moons and other bodies in the solar system then formed out of the remaining material, around 4,600 million years ago.

As the earth took shape, heavier (denser) elements sank towards the centre. Lighter elements tended to rise towards the surface. As a result, the earth is layered into zones of varying density (which scientists measure in grams per cubic centimetre).

The least dense zone, the crust, has two distinct parts. The lighter continental crust has a density of 2.7. Its average thickness is 35 to 40 km, though under the highest mountain ranges it reaches 70 km thick. The oceanic crust, which forms most of the ocean floor and which lies under the continental crust, averages only 6 km in thickness. It has a density of 3.0.

Underlying the crust is the mantle, which is about 2,900 km thick. Its density ranges from 3.4 near the top to 5.8 lower down. The mantle encloses the core. This consists of an outer, liquid core with an average density of between 9.4 and 12, and a solid inner core with a density of 13.54.

While the earth's crust is composed mostly of light elements, the earth's core consists mainly of iron. Evidence for this comes from meteorites. Light and stony meteorites are probably fragments of the crust of some ancient planet. Other meteorites are heavy and composed mainly of iron and nickel. They may be fragments of a planet's core.

The earth is divided into three main zones: the crust, mantle and core. These zones are distinguished by their density, which increases between the light, stony crust and the dense, metallic core. The core, mantle and crust are also divided into zones. The diagram, below, shows that the crust has two main zones. The continental crust is called sial, because it is rich in silica (a substance formed from silicon and oxygen) and aluminium. The oceanic crust is called sima, because it is rich in silica and magnesium. The sima, which lies under the continental crust, is denser than the sial. Beneath the oceanic crust is the mantle, the top part of which is solid. This layer, together with the crust, forms a solid shell around the earth called the lithosphere. The lithosphere is cracked into large sections called plates. Under the lithosphere is a semi-molten layer of the mantle, called the asthenosphere. Movements in the liquid asthenosphere make the plates move around, causing continental drift. Continental drift has probably been going on throughout earth history, forever changing the face of the earth.

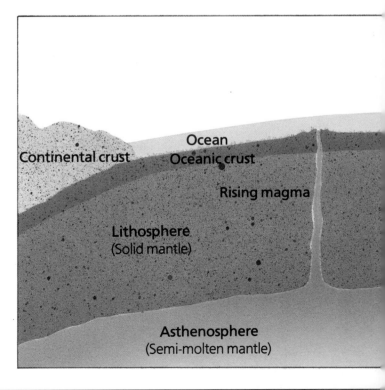

Continental crust
Ocean
Oceanic crust
Rising magma
Lithosphere (Solid mantle)
Asthenosphere (Semi-molten mantle)

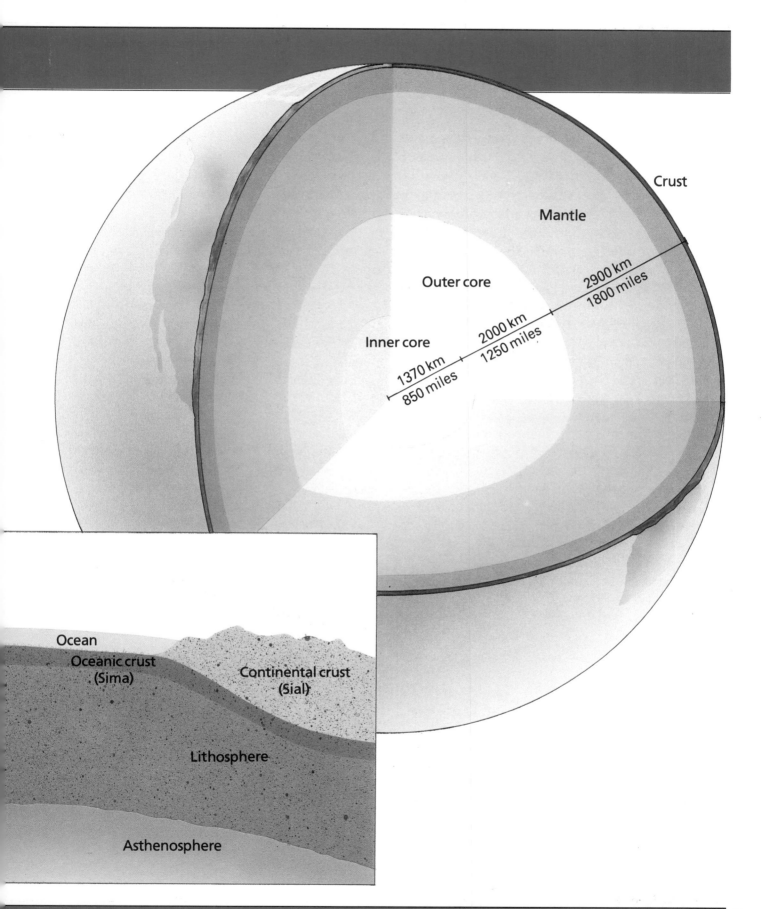

The changing earth

For millions of years after its formation, the earth's surface was probably molten. Whenever parts of the surface cooled and hardened, they were cracked and re-melted by the heat below. As a result, the oldest rocks found so far on earth are only about 3,800 million years old, though some crystals of a rare metal called zirconium, found in rocks in Australia, have been dated at 4,200 million years old. Yet the oldest Moon rocks and meteorites are about 4,600 million years old. They were formed, most scientists believe, at the same time as earth.

Eventually, the crust began to cool and harden. Volcanoes, which have been active throughout earth history, released gases and water vapour from the rocks. These substances formed an early atmosphere around the earth. Storms raged and water vapour fell to the surface as rain. As the surface cooled, water collected in hollows to form the first seas.

The creation of an atmosphere started a number of processes which eroded, or wore away, surface rocks. The earth's surface, unlike that of the Moon which has no atmosphere, has been constantly changing ever since.

Some of the processes involved in erosion are called weathering. Mechanical weathering occurs when frost action or rapid heating and cooling shatter rocks. Chemical weathering occurs, for

In the early days of earth history, our planet's surface was probably molten, looking much like this lava lake in Hawaii.

example, when rainwater containing dissolved carbon dioxide eats away at limestone, wearing out huge caves.

Running water, especially fast-flowing rivers, wears out deep, V-shaped valleys, while glaciers (moving bodies of ice) gouge out U-shaped troughs. Along coasts, storm waves batter the shore and currents sweep away eroded rocks. In deserts, the main force of erosion is the wind. Strong winds act like natural sand-blasters when they hurl sand grains against exposed rocks and gradually wear them away.

Above Franz Josef Glacier in the Southern Alps, New Zealand.

Factors in erosion

1. Weathering (Snow, rain and sun)
2. Running water (Rivers etc)
3. Wind
4. Coastal
5. Glaciation
6. Chemical action

Geological time

Until the mid-nineteenth century, many people thought that the earth was only a few thousand years old. But geologists, who studied how rocks were formed and changed by natural forces, began to realize that the earth must be far older. Scientists who studied fossils (traces of ancient life in rocks) began to understand that they were a record of life on earth. Such people thought, but could not prove, that the earth must be millions of years old.

The discovery of radioactivity at the end of the nineteenth century finally enabled scientists to date rocks. This is because radioactive substances, such as uranium, disintegrate (decay) at a fixed rate. When uranium disintegrates, it leaves lead as an end product. Hence, by measuring the proportion of lead in a uranium sample, scientists can calculate its age and the age of the rock in which it occurs.

Geologists have divided earth history into six eras. The Azoic, Archeozoic and Proterozoic eras cover the bulk of earth history, while the last 570 million years are divided into the Paleozoic, Mesozoic and Cenozoic eras. These three eras are divided into periods. For example, the Paleozoic contains six periods, starting with the Cambrian period. Cambrian rocks are the first in earth history in which fossils are common. Because Azoic, Archeozoic and Proterozoic rocks contain so few fossils, we know little about the evolution of life in these eras. As a result, they are often grouped together and simply called the Pre-Cambrian.

Right The geological time scale covering the last 570 million years is divided into three eras. The eras are divided into periods and some periods are divided into epochs. The figures on the right show how long ago the era, period, or epoch began in millions of years. The Paleozoic era began 570 million years ago, the Mesozoic era began 230 million years ago, and the Cenozoic era began 65 million years ago. The Pre-Cambrian is a vast expanse of time, stretching from 570 million years ago back to the formation of the earth.

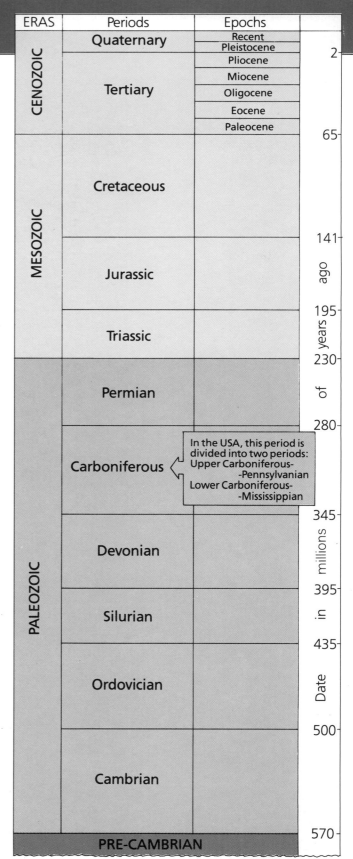

ERAS	Periods	Epochs	Date in millions of years ago
CENOZOIC	Quaternary	Recent	
		Pleistocene	2
	Tertiary	Pliocene	
		Miocene	
		Oligocene	
		Eocene	
		Paleocene	
MESOZOIC	Cretaceous		65
	Jurassic		141
	Triassic		195
PALEOZOIC	Permian		230
	Carboniferous		280
	Devonian		345
	Silurian		395
	Ordovician		435
	Cambrian		500
PRE-CAMBRIAN			570

In the USA, this period is divided into two periods: Upper Carboniferous- -Pennsylvanian Lower Carboniferous- -Mississippian

The era covering the last two million years is the Cenozoic. It consists of the Tertiary period, which is divided into five epochs and the Quaternary period. The Quaternary period contains the Pleistocene epoch, when a great Ice Age occurred, and the Recent (or Holocene) epoch, which covers the last few thousand years.

Above During the last great Ice Age, large parts of the northern hemisphere, which are now ice-free, resembled the icy continent of Antarctica.

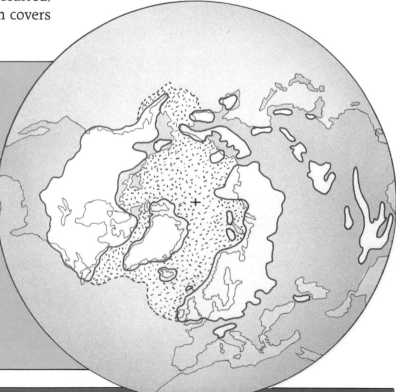

The map shows the greatest extent of the ice sheets in the northern hemisphere during the Pleistocene epoch. There were several glacial stages, when the ice spread over large areas. Between the glacial stages, there were interglacial stages when it was often warmer than it is today. The ice then melted and the sea-level rose. Some experts think that we are now living in an interglacial stage. When this stage ends, the ice sheets may return to cover New York City, Chicago, London, Berlin and Moscow.

Kinds of rocks

There are three main kinds of rocks: igneous, sedimentary and metamorphic. Igneous rocks are formed from molten material, called magma. Sedimentary rocks are formed from sediments (fragments of other rocks and the remains of once-living organisms), or by chemical action. Metamorphic rocks are formed when heat and pressure metamorphose (change) igneous and sedimentary rocks (see page 18).

Some igneous rocks are said to be extrusive, because the magma is extruded (forced to the surface) through volcanoes or fissures (cracks). There it is called lava. The three main types of lava are ropy lava or *pahoehoe* (a Hawaiian word); rough block lava, or *aa*, pronounced 'ah-ah'; and pillow lava, formed on sea-beds.

Extrusive igneous rocks include basalt, which makes up many oceanic islands and such rock features as the Giant's Causeway in Northern Ireland. The second most abundant rock formed from lava is andesite, which is named after the Andes Mountains in South America. Other similar rocks are rhyolite and trachyte. Extrusive igneous rocks are usually fine-grained — that is, they consist of tiny particles. This is because extruded magma cools quickly and mineral crystals have no time to form. One kind of rock formed by rapid cooling, obsidian, has a glassy texture.

When volcanoes erupt, magma is often exploded into the air. Rocks formed from such particles are called pyroclasts. They include sizeable lumps of magma called volcanic bombs and smaller particles called lapilli. Another pyroclast is pumice, a lightweight rock with a honeycomb structure. It is formed from frothy lava containing gas bubbles.

Rocks formed from particles of fine volcanic ash are called tuff. Ignimbrite is similar. It is formed from clouds of hot gas and ash, called *nuées ardentes*, which is French for 'glowing clouds'. When the ash settles, the hot particles are welded together into a solid mass.

The Giant's Causeway in Northern Ireland is made up of basalt, an extrusive igneous rock, which formed from lava on the surface.

Above Ignimbrite is often quarried and used as a building stone.
Right A section through a volcano.

1. Reservoir of magma
2. Volcano's central vent
3. Side vents
4. Ash
5. Lava flows
6. Alternate layers of ash and lava

11

Intrusive igneous rocks

Much of the magma which rises into the crust never reaches the surface. Instead, it solidifies underground. Rocks formed from this magma are called intrusive igneous rocks, because the magma has intruded (forced its way) into existing rocks.

Some intrusive igneous rocks form in sheets, called dykes, which cut across existing rock layers. Other sheets, called sills, run parallel to existing rock layers. Laccoliths are similar to sills, but they are much larger and often arch up overlying rocks. Batholiths are the largest bodies of intrusive igneous rocks. They are usually formed at the same time as mountains and they often cover thousands of square kilometres. The most common rock in batholiths is granite. For example, batholiths were formed during the uplift of the Eastern Uplands of

Right This dyke in Spain was formed when magma was forced through existing rock layers.

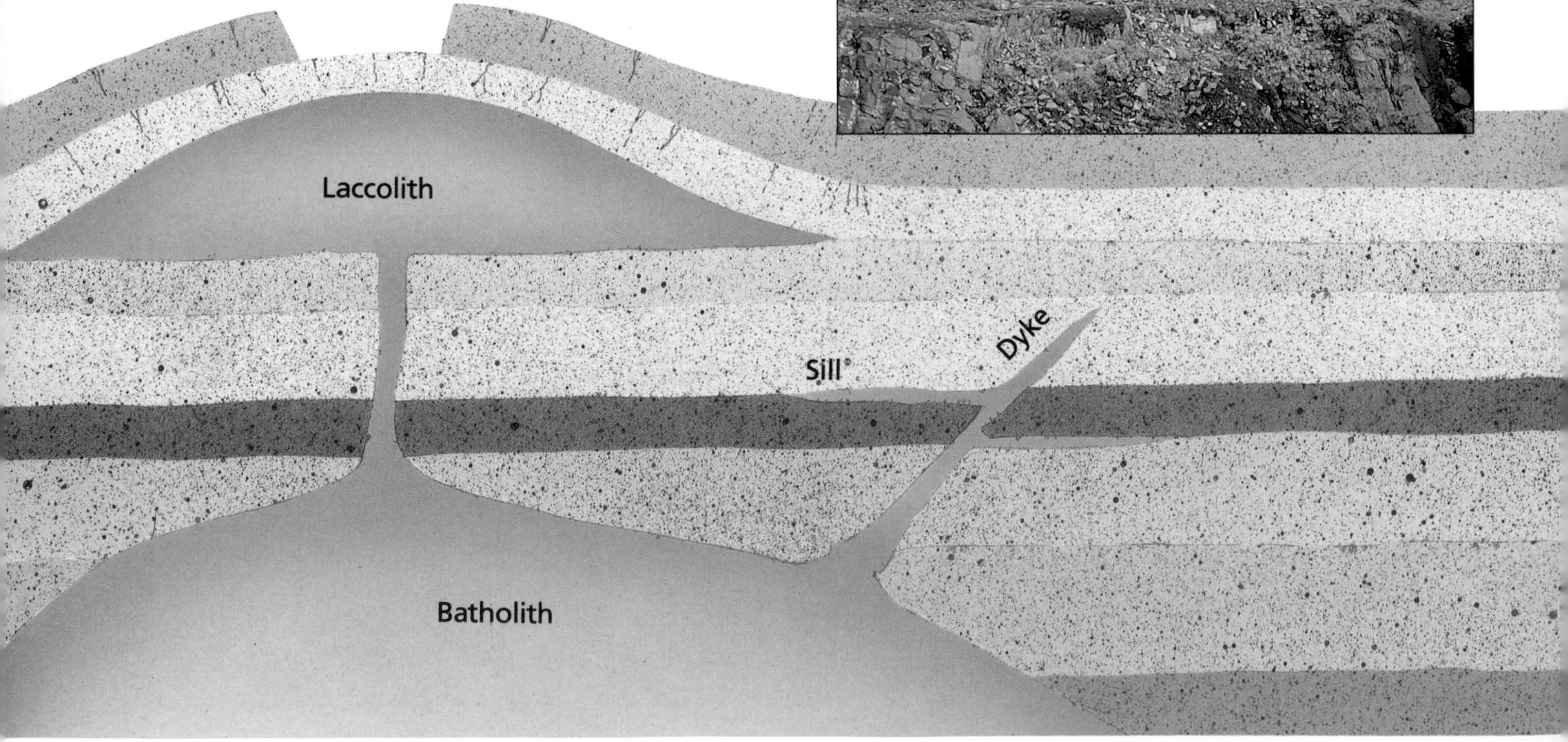

Laccolith

Sill

Dyke

Batholith

Australia and the Sierra Nevada range in the western USA. The batholiths were formed 16 km or more below the surface. As the mountains rose upwards, the overlying rocks were eroded away and parts of the batholiths have been exposed.

Intrusive igneous rocks are medium-grained to coarse-grained in texture. The mineral grains in coarse-grained rocks are more than 1–2 mm across, as compared with fine-grained extrusive igneous rocks, composed of particles less than 0.1 mm across. Granites look mottled, because the mineral grains can be seen with the naked eye. Granite consists mainly of feldspars, (a group of minerals which may be grey, pink or white), and quartz, which resembles glass. Often dark grains of hornblende and mica are also visible.

Another intrusive igneous rock, chemically similar to granite, is called pegmatite. But pegmatites contain large crystals, which are several centimetres across. Pegmatites form after the main body of granite has solidified and so they cool very slowly. They often contain less common minerals. Other intrusive rocks include diorite, gabbro, serpentinite and syenite.

Above This granite outcrop is on Dartmoor, England. Granite, the most common intrusive igneous rock, forms underground from huge masses of hot magma, which cool and harden. It appears on the surface when the overlying rocks are worn away. The granite is weathered into shapes resembling pieces of modern sculpture.

Opposite The diagram shows various bodies of intrusive igneous rocks. The largest are batholiths.

Right In the centre of this picture is a piece of granite. Granite occurs in several colours. This black and white sample is made up mainly of four common minerals. From left to right, they are mica, quartz, horneblende and feldspar.

Sedimentary rocks

Many sedimentary rocks are clastic — that is, they consist of broken fragments of other rocks, including pebbles, sand, silt, mud and dust. These fragments are transported by running water, glaciers and the wind. They are finally deposited, usually in water, where the loose grains are compacted and cemented together. They then form such rocks as sandstones, siltstones, mudstones and shale. The 'cement' which binds the loose grains together consists of minerals precipitated, or dropped, from water which seeps through the sediments. Such natural cements include the minerals anhydrite, calcite, dolomite and iron oxides, which stain the sediments red.

Sedimentary rocks form in layers, or strata. These vary from less than 1 cm to several metres thick. The strata are often almost horizontal, because they form on flat, or gently sloping lake and sea floors. Between one layer and another is a distinct line, or bedding plane. But on exposed cliffs, you will often see folded or tilted strata. They are the result of earth movements. Sandstones, formed in deserts, may be cross-bedded — that is, one layer lies obliquely (at an angle) to the layers above and below it. Cross-bedding is caused by variable winds in deserts or sometimes by variable currents in water.

Conglomerates (also called puddingstones) are clastic sedimentary rocks. They consist of rounded pebbles cemented in fine silt or sand (called the matrix). Breccias are similar, except that the larger fragments are jagged and angular. Tillites consist

Left Cross-bedded sandstones are exposed in Antelope Canyon in northern Arizona, USA. Cross-bedding is a feature of sandstones formed from ancient desert sand dunes. They are also formed when variable currents in water sweep sand grains back and forth.

Above These layers of sandstones and siltstones in Iran were once flat. They have been tilted by earth movements.

of sizeable rocks set in fine 'rock flour'. They are formed from rock fragments transported by glaciers.

Sandstones are medium-grained rocks, made up mainly of quartz. Siltstones, mudstones and shale are fine-grained sedimentary rocks. Loess, formed from wind-blown silt and dust, is also fine-grained.

Many sedimentary rocks contain fossils. Fossil-rich rocks have played a vital role in unravelling the complex story of life on earth.

Far left Conglomerates are coarse-grained sedimentary rocks. They consist of pebbles cemented into fine silt or sand.

Left Sandstone is a medium-grained sedimentary rock. It is made up of grains of sand which have been cemented together by minerals deposited from water.

Chemical and organic rocks

There are two other groups of sedimentary rocks. One group is formed by chemical action. The other consists of rocks made up of organic (once-living) matter.

One common sedimentary rock, limestone, is made up mostly of the mineral calcite. It may be of clastic, chemical or organic origin. For example, broken fragments of limestone cemented together form a clastic rock called limestone breccia.

Other limestones, such as stalactites and stalagmites, are formed by chemical action, when calcite is precipitated from water draining through caves. Travertine is similar. It is precipitated from water in hot springs. Oolitic limestone is formed by chemical action on sea floors. It consists of masses of tiny, round grains, resembling fish roe. Each grain consists of layers of calcite which have been precipitated around bits of sand or shell.

One of the purest forms of limestone, chalk, consists of the microscopic remains of marine plants and animals. Coral limestones are also mainly organic in origin. They consist of layer upon layer of the hard external skeletons of tiny animals called polyps. Shelly limestones consist largely of fossil shells.

Cherts and flints, often found as nodules (lumps) in chalk formations, are also sometimes precipitated from water which is rich in silica. Some chemically formed rocks are called evaporites. For example, rock salt forms when seas evaporate. Another evaporite, gypsum, is used to make plaster of Paris.

Calcite is precipitated from water in limestone caves to form hanging stalactites and column-like stalagmites.

Left Cleopatra Terrace is at Mammoth Hot Springs in Yellowstone National Park, in Wyoming in the USA. It consists of a mineral called travertine, which is mostly calcite. The travertine is precipitated from the water which flows from a large hot spring.

Organic rocks include coal, which is a fossil fuel, consisting of the remains of land plants. Coal goes through a number of stages. Peat represents an early stage. It has a high water content. Gradually, the water is squeezed out and the peat is compressed into brown coal or lignite. Further compression turns the lignite into bituminous coal and eventually into anthracite. Anthracite, the final stage in coal formation, is hard and shiny.

Metamorphic rocks

Just as wet dough is transformed by heat into bread, so igneous and sedimentary rocks can be changed, or metamorphosed, so that their appearance and character are completely altered.

There are several kinds of metamorphic processes. Dynamic metamorphism is the result of intense pressure, whilst contact metamorphism is caused by great heat. Regional metamorphism, involving both pressure and heat, occurs during mountain building periods, when rocks are folded and huge pockets of magma form in the crust. Around huge bodies of magma (batholiths), a zone of rocks up to three kilometres wide may be metamorphosed. No chemical changes occur during metamorphism, unless new minerals are introduced by chemically active fluids. This process is called metasomatism.

During metamorphism, the existing minerals are often recrystallized or rearranged. For example, when soft shale is metamorphosed to become hard slate, the minerals in the rock are rearranged in layers. This gives slate its chief characteristic — its ability to split into thin sheets which are used as roof tiles. Other metamorphic rocks, called gneisses, often show irregular bands caused by mineral realignment.

Marble is formed when limestone or a similar rock, dolomite, is subjected to dynamic and regional metamorphism. Snowy-white marble, which takes a high polish, is prized by sculptors. But marble may also be coloured evenly, or in patches or bands, by impurities. Coloured marble is often used to floor or face the walls of public buildings.

Opposite Marble of superb quality is quarried at Carrara in northern Italy. It has been used by many sculptors to make works of art, including this statue adorning a fountain in Rome.

Left Slate is formed when soft shales or sometimes mudstones and tuff are metamorphosed (changed) by heat and pressure. This slate quarry is in North Wales, UK, where the slate is split into roof tiles.

Other metamorphic rocks include hornfels, a hard rock formed by contact metamorphism; mica schist, formed when mudstones and siltstones are subjected to regional metamorphism; and quartzite, formed when sandstones made up mainly of quartz are subjected to contact and regional metamorphism. Inexperienced rock collectors may find it hard to distinguish some metamorphic rocks from igneous rocks.

Rocks and scenery

The study of rocks helps us to understand the origin of land forms and scenery. Sedimentary rocks are especially important, because they cover about 75 per cent of the world's land surfaces, even though they make up only 5 per cent of the top 16 km of the earth's crust.

One of the chief factors affecting scenery is the relative hardness of rock strata and their resistance to erosion. For example, resistant rocks, such as granite or limestone, stand out as headlands on coasts. But outcrops of shale, siltstones and mudstones are more easily eroded to form bays.

Many igneous rocks resist erosion. Granite outcrops often form rugged upland landscapes and *inselbergs* — isolated, steep-sided hills. The necks of old volcanoes, called plugs, also form steep-sided hills, such as Devils Tower, in the United States. Basalt, formed from lava, often contracts as it cools, forming clusters of six-sided columns. This produces such spectacular features as the Giant's Causeway, in Northern Ireland.

Some massive types of limestone are especially hard. They form ranges of hills, while softer shales and mudstones are worn down into valleys. Karst scenery, named after a district in Yugoslavia, is a feature of limestone uplands. Massive limestone contains lines of weaknesses, namely a network of vertical cracks and horizontal bedding planes,

Devils Tower National Monument, in South Dakota, USA, is the remains of a plug, or neck, of an ancient volcano.

through which water can seep. Rainwater containing dissolved carbon dioxide is a weak acid. It enlarges the cracks and bedding planes, creating tunnels and caves. Many limestone surfaces are rocky and lack soil. Rain usually flows directly into holes in the rock, leaving the surface dry. Few plants are able to grow.

Many sandstones also resist erosion. In places, such as Monument Valley in the southwestern United States, horizontal sandstone strata form flat-topped hills called mesas. The sandstone rests upon and protects layers of softer shales.

Left Limestone surfaces are worn into blocks called clints, separated by fissures called grikes.

Below Hard sandstones cap the steep-sided mesas in Monument Valley in the USA.

Kinds of minerals

Rocks are made up of minerals. But minerals, unlike rocks, have a definite chemical composition and formula. Scientists have identified nearly 3,000 different minerals.

Minerals consist of elements, 92 of which occur naturally in the earth's crust. Of these, 22 sometimes occur in a pure or nearly pure state. These native or free elements include gold and silver. Copper and iron also occur (rarely) as native elements, but most of the copper and iron used in industry comes from mineral ores. Ores are chemical combinations of the metallic element with others, such as oxygen and sulphur.

Some native elements occur in more than one form. For example, pure carbon occurs as the soft native element, graphite, and also as diamond, the hardest natural substance. The reason why these forms of carbon are so different lies in the structural arrangement of the atoms in the minerals.

Above Crystals of smoky quartz.

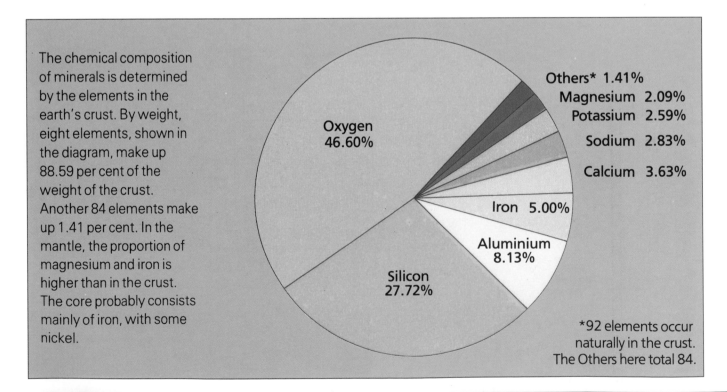

The chemical composition of minerals is determined by the elements in the earth's crust. By weight, eight elements, shown in the diagram, make up 88.59 per cent of the weight of the crust. Another 84 elements make up 1.41 per cent. In the mantle, the proportion of magnesium and iron is higher than in the crust. The core probably consists mainly of iron, with some nickel.

Oxygen 46.60%

Others* 1.41%
Magnesium 2.09%
Potassium 2.59%
Sodium 2.83%
Calcium 3.63%

Iron 5.00%

Aluminium 8.13%

Silicon 27.72%

*92 elements occur naturally in the crust. The Others here total 84.

Above Muscovite is a form of the mineral mica. When struck with a hammer, muscovite splits into thin, transparent sheets. These sheets were once used in Moscow as windowpanes. Mica is a silicate which is rich in aluminium. It is a rock-forming mineral.

All minerals are inorganic (lifeless) substances. Most of them are chemical combinations of two or more elements. For example, the chemical formula of galena, an ore of lead, is PbS. This means that galena is a chemical combination of lead (Pb) and sulphur (S).

Two elements, oxygen and silicon, account for 74.32 per cent of the weight of the earth's crust. Six more — aluminium, iron, calcium, sodium, potassium and magnesium — make up another 24.27 per cent. The remaining 84 elements make up the balance.

The most common minerals, called silicates, are chemical combinations of oxygen and silicon, often with one or more of the other common elements. The silicates include quartz and several groups of minerals called feldspars, micas, olivines and pyroxenes. Silicates are so common that they are called rock-forming minerals. For example, a sample of granite is composed almost entirely of silicates (see pages 12–13). Calcite is another rock-forming mineral. It makes up most of limestone and dolomite (see page 16).

Left These calcite crystals are called dog-tooth spar because of their pointed, triangular shapes. Calcite is a common, rock-forming mineral. Calcite crystals are common, but their shapes vary greatly.

Minerals in industry

While rock-forming minerals are common, geologists have to search for minerals used in industry and in jewellery. The search for minerals requires a knowledge of how they are formed. For example, when igneous rocks form, the common silicates harden first. Mineral-rich fluids are left over. Some cool in cavities in the rock while others are forced into joints and fissures, to form veins. Other valuable minerals, such as garnets, are formed when rocks are metamorphosed. Some eroded fragments of minerals, including diamonds and gold, are found in sedimentary deposits, such as river gravels.

Many ores are mined. For example, bauxite yields the useful metal aluminium. Bauxite is the name for a group of minerals formed in tropical regions when heavy rain reacts with rocks containing aluminium silicates. The silicates are removed by water action and various minerals (aluminium oxides), are left behind.

Copper ores include chalcopyrite, which is yellow in appearance; azurite, which is always blue; malachite, which may occur in beautiful bands of green; and cuprite, which is red. However, mineral collectors should remember that colour can be misleading when identifying minerals. Because of impurities and the effects of such things as heat, light and chemical action, many minerals occur in a wide range of colours.

Common iron ores include hematite, a grey to black mineral, and magnetite, which is also dark in colour. But if you scratch hematite, you produce a red powder. This powder is called the streak. By contrast, the streak of magnetite is black.

The chief ore of lead is galena, which often occurs in veins with sphalerite, the main ore of zinc. The chief tin ore is cassiterite, which is often found with sphalerite and wolframite (tungsten ore). The mineral uraninite is the ore of the radioactive element uranium.

Below Chalcopyrite is a copper-iron sulphide, which is often called fool's gold.

Below Gold may be found in a pure or almost pure state often with quartz as in this pebble.

Pyrite, or iron sulphide, is a pale, brassy-yellow mineral which, because of its appearance, is often called fool's gold. But pyrite is both harder and more brittle than gold. Gold also has a high specific gravity of 19.3. This means that a sample of gold is 19.3 times as heavy as the same volume of water. Pyrite, on the other hand, has a specific gravity of 5.0. Powdered pyrite dissolves in nitric acid. But only *aqua regia*, a mixture of concentrated nitric and hydrochloric acid, will dissolve gold.

Right Azurite is a beautiful blue mineral. It is one of the ores of copper.

Below Mining for gold at Dawson City in the Yukon, Canada. Dawson City attracted thousands of hopeful prospectors during the Klondike gold rush of 1897–8.

Precious minerals

The popularity of birthstones and the belief that they bring good luck reveals the fascination that rare and beautiful stones have exerted on people ever since the Stone Age. The most prized gemstones are diamonds (birthstones for April). They are formed at great depths and under tremendous pressure in a rock called kimberlite (blue ground). The brilliant sparkle of cut diamonds, together with their durability, are features which make them so popular.

Another stone, the red ruby (birthstone for July), is often more expensive than diamond. Ruby and the cornflower-blue sapphire (birthstone for September) are varieties of a dull, hard mineral, corundum. Another prized gem is emerald, birthstone for May. It is a transparent, green variety of the mineral beryl.

Many semiprecious stones are varieties of silica. For example, coloured varieties of quartz, such as purple amethyst and yellow citrine, are used in jewellery. Another form of silica, chalcedony, is composed of minute quartz crystals. Flint, lumps of which are found in chalk, is a common form of chalcedony, while semiprecious forms include reddish carnelian, red jasper, green chrysoprase and a banded mineral called agate. Opals also belong to the silica group. They are prized for their opalescence — that is, they display the colours of the rainbow when rotated. This effect occurs because light is split up by the internal structure of the mineral.

Sky-blue turquoise is another popular gemstone, as also is spinel, a red variety of which resembles ruby. Alexandrite, a type of chrysoberyl, has an interesting characteristic. It is green in natural light and red in artificial light. Zircons are sometimes used instead of diamonds, although they often chip at the edges. Garnets occur in many colours, while jadeite (jade) is usually green or greenish white. The Chinese, in particular, have made superb jade ornaments.

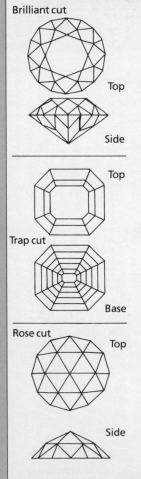

Various cuts are used to show off the properties of gemstones. The brilliant cut is used for top-quality diamonds. In this cut, the stone is usually given 58 facets (inclined sides), though some stones have more. Light entering the diamond from the top is reflected back by the rear facets. This gives the stone its sparkle and play of colours, called fire. The diagram shows the top and side view of the brilliant cut. The trap, or step, cut is used for emeralds and aquamarines. The rose cut is often used for small diamonds or those of a lower quality.

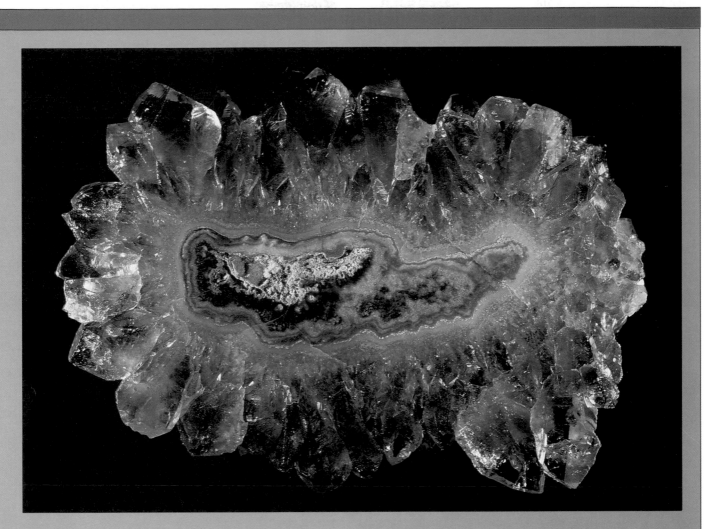

Above Amethyst is a purple form of quartz. Its name comes from a Greek word meaning unintoxicated. People once thought that amethyst stopped them becoming drunk.

Opposite above Cut diamonds are highly prized gemstones.

Right Some of the world's finest opals are mined at Coober Pedy in southern Australia.

How fossils are formed

A few hundred years ago, some scholars argued that the resemblance of fossils to plants and animals was accidental. Others thought that the Devil had put them in rocks to confuse people. But by the late seventeenth century, there were scientists who understood that fossils were evidence of ancient life.

For fossils to form, animals and plants must be quickly buried by sediment. If this does not happen, they soon disintegrate. After burial, the soft parts of the organisms decay, but the harder parts, such as bones and shells, are preserved. Eventually, as the sediments are slowly compressed into sedimentary rocks, water seeping downwards may dissolve these hard parts, leaving hollow forms, or moulds, of the original. The moulds are often later filled by minerals precipitated from water. This creates fossil casts.

Moulds and casts preserve the shape, but not the internal features of the original. Sometimes, however, minerals are deposited in the pores, or tiny holes, of a buried specimen, such as a bone. As cells in the bone are dissolved away, they, too, are replaced by minerals. This slow process is called permineralization. It creates a stone copy, or petrified version, of the original. For example, each cell in a petrified log has been replaced by minerals. Every detail of the original wood is visible.

Leaves are preserved as carbon smears, formed when buried leaves are converted into carbon. There is also a group of trace fossils. They include petrified animal droppings, footprints and eggs.

A few fossils are the actual bodies of ancient creatures. For example, insects are trapped in drops of sticky tree resin which harden eventually into lumps of transparent amber. In the Ice Age, woolly mammoths were buried in swamps which froze. Entombed in the frozen soil, their flesh has been preserved for thousands of years.

Opposite These petrified tree trunks in Yellowstone National Park in the USA are replicas in stone of trees which grew millions of years ago.

Below This spider was preserved in amber about 38 million years ago.

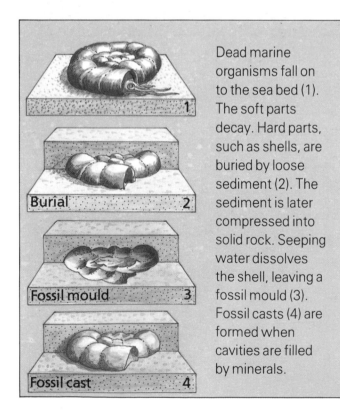

Dead marine organisms fall on to the sea bed (1). The soft parts decay. Hard parts, such as shells, are buried by loose sediment (2). The sediment is later compressed into solid rock. Seeping water dissolves the shell, leaving a fossil mould (3). Fossil casts (4) are formed when cavities are filled by minerals.

Fossils and evolution

Mystery surrounds the origins and early development of life on earth. This is because fossils in Pre-Cambrian rocks are rare. The oldest fossils — of bacteria and single-celled algae (simple plants) — are dated at 3,500 million years old. However, the first rocks in which fossils are common are those of the Cambrian period, which began 570 million years ago.

From the emergence of primitive fishes (the first vertebrates, or animals with backbones) in the late Cambrian period, the fossil record shows how increasingly complex life forms have developed. The procession of life on earth is still a matter of dispute. Some people accept the Biblical version of the Creation. Others have suggested that major changes are the result of catastrophes, or disasters, which cause mass extinctions of species.

Today most scientists accept Charles Darwin's theory of gradual evolution. Darwin (1809–82) put forward the idea of natural selection. This stated that any species possessing certain features which gave it an advantage over other species stood a greater chance of survival. The fossil record shows how many species alive today might have developed from long-extinct ancestors. But there are many gaps in the record.

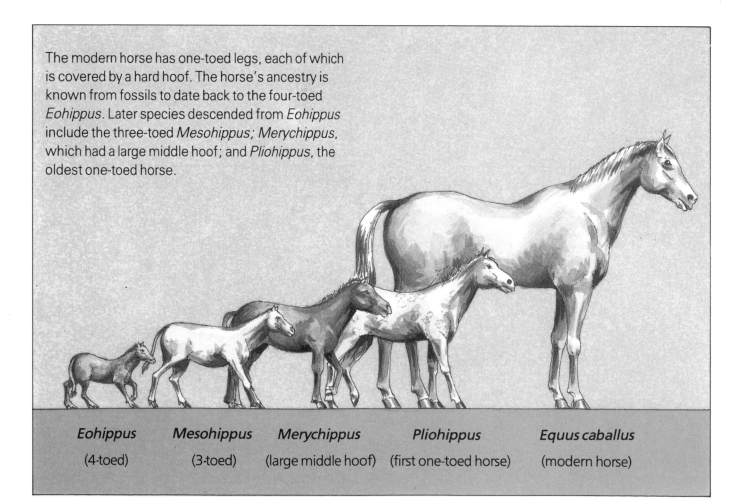

The modern horse has one-toed legs, each of which is covered by a hard hoof. The horse's ancestry is known from fossils to date back to the four-toed *Eohippus*. Later species descended from *Eohippus* include the three-toed *Mesohippus*; *Merychippus*, which had a large middle hoof; and *Pliohippus*, the oldest one-toed horse.

Eohippus	*Mesohippus*	*Merychippus*	*Pliohippus*	*Equus caballus*
(4-toed)	(3-toed)	(large middle hoof)	(first one-toed horse)	(modern horse)

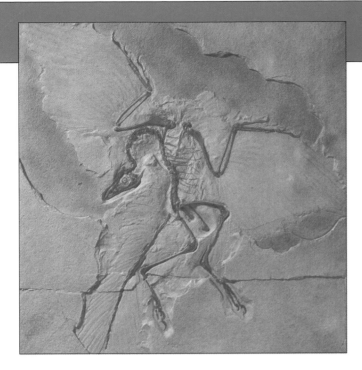

Left *Archaeopteryx* lived in the Jurassic period. Geologists believe that it was a bird, because fossils show that it had feathers. *Archaeopteryx* also had many reptilian features. As a result, most scientists believe that birds evolved from reptiles.

Earth history

It is difficult to comprehend the true length of time involved in earth history. One way to understand this is to imagine all of earth time compressed into 12 hours. For the first hour and a half, the earth's surface is mainly molten. The oldest fossil traces of bacteria and algae are alive at 2.52 am. The Cambrian period starts at 10.30 am. The first vertebrates appear at about 10.40 am and the first amphibians at about 11.00 am (in the Devonian period). The earliest creatures which might have been our primitive ancestors do not appear until about 37 seconds before noon. On this 12-hour scale, all of recorded history can be compressed into less than a twentieth of a second.

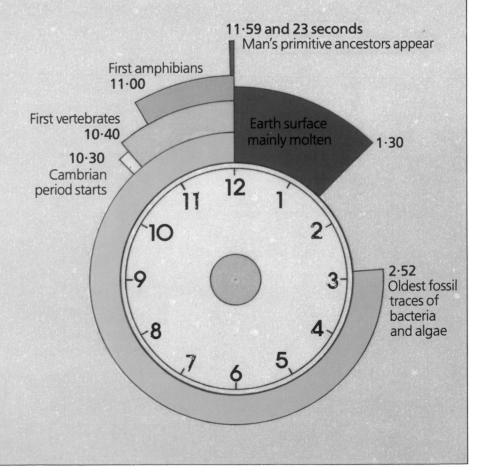

Reading the rocks

Fossils not only help geologists to unravel the complex story of life on earth, they also help in the dating of rock strata.

In the early nineteenth century, a British engineer, William Smith, was supervising the building of canals. As the workmen cut through sedimentary rocks, Smith collected fossils from the various layers. Some fossils appeared in layer after layer of rock. Others, called index fossils, were confined to one layer. Smith realized that these fossils were the remains of organisms which had evolved and died out during the formation of that rock layer. Providing that such fossils are found over large areas, they can be used to establish that certain rock layers, however far apart, are of the same age.

Smith also realized that in undisturbed rocks the lower layers are older than the layers above them. Smith then worked out the sequence of rocks in southern England and their relative ages. But their absolute ages could not be fixed until the discovery of radioactivity (see page 8). By mapping where the layers appeared at the surface, Smith compiled the world's first geological map in 1815.

The study of rock strata is called stratigraphy. Sedimentary rocks and the fossils they contain provide much information about the climate when the rocks were formed. For example, limestones containing coral remains were formed in warm, shallow seas, while coal was formed in warm swamps. The fact that coal is found in Antarctica shows that the climate of that icy continent was once much warmer than it is today.

The study of rock strata and rock structures, including folds and faults (cracks along which rocks have moved) is also important in prospecting and finding water-bearing rock layers. These can be tapped by wells.

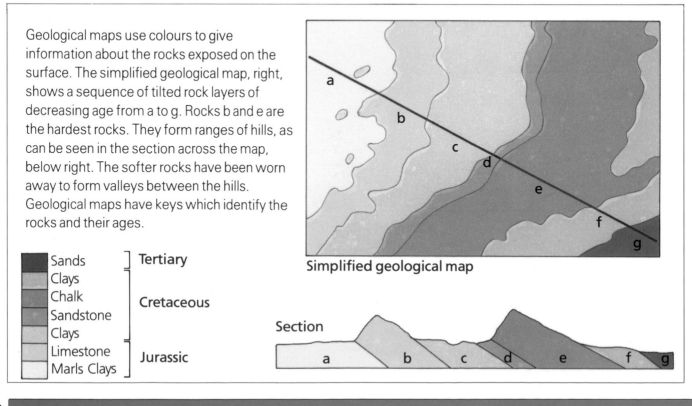

Geological maps use colours to give information about the rocks exposed on the surface. The simplified geological map, right, shows a sequence of tilted rock layers of decreasing age from a to g. Rocks b and e are the hardest rocks. They form ranges of hills, as can be seen in the section across the map, below right. The softer rocks have been worn away to form valleys between the hills. Geological maps have keys which identify the rocks and their ages.

Simplified geological map

	Rock	Period
	Sands	Tertiary
	Clays	
	Chalk	Cretaceous
	Sandstone	
	Clays	
	Limestone	Jurassic
	Marls Clays	

Section

The walls of the Grand Canyon, in the USA, cover a slice of earth history, from Pre-Cambrian rocks at the very bottom to Permian rocks at the top. The section shows the main rock layers.

Permian

Carboniferous

Cambrian

Pre-Cambrian

Scale: 1.5 cm to 1 km (1 inch to 1 mile) (horizontal and vertical)

Ancient life

The word *Paleozoic* means 'ancient life'. The Paleozoic era includes six periods. However, American geologists divide one of them, the Carboniferous, into two parts. They call the first part the Mississippian period and the second part the Pennsylvanian period.

The reason why Pre-Cambrian rocks contain so few fossils is probably that living organisms, including jellyfish and worms, were soft-bodied. But at the start of the Cambrian period, many animals had hard parts. They included brachiopods (shelled animals related to worms); graptolites, colonial animals which are useful index fossils; sponges; and trilobites. Trilobites are distinctive fossils which are common in Paleozoic rocks. (They

became extinct in the Permian period.) The late Cambrian period saw the appearance of the first cephalopods (molluscs with tentacles) and, about 510 million years ago, primitive jawless and toothless fish, called *agnathans*. They are the first known vertebrates. Fossil fragments of their scales have been found in Wyoming, in the USA.

Fish increased in numbers in the Ordovician and Silurian periods. During the Silurian period, some marine creatures, such as giant sea scorpions, reached a large size. The Silurian period was the first in which plants spread on to the land.

The Devonian period saw the development of many forms of fish, including cartilaginous fish, the ancestors of sharks and rays. Some fish belonged to

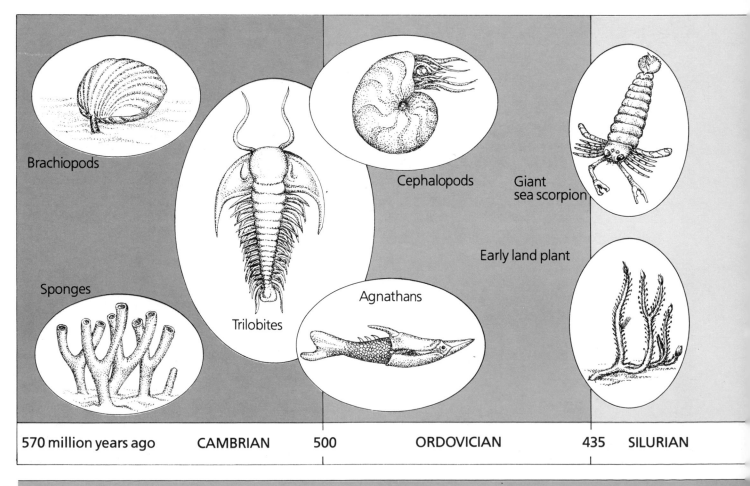

Brachiopods

Cephalopods

Giant sea scorpion

Early land plant

Sponges

Agnathans

Trilobites

| 570 million years ago | CAMBRIAN | 500 | ORDOVICIAN | 435 | SILURIAN |

another important group, the lungfish, which could breathe in air when coastal waters dried up. They are thought to be the ancestors of the first amphibians, which appeared in the Devonian period about 350 million years ago.

The Carboniferous period saw the development of large forests of giant clubmosses, fern trees and horsetails, whose remains survive today in coal beds around the world. The earliest reptiles developed in the late Carboniferous and Permian periods.

Left Trilobites are useful index fossils, because they help geologists to fix the date of Paleozoic rocks.
Below Evolutionary highlights in the Paleozoic era.

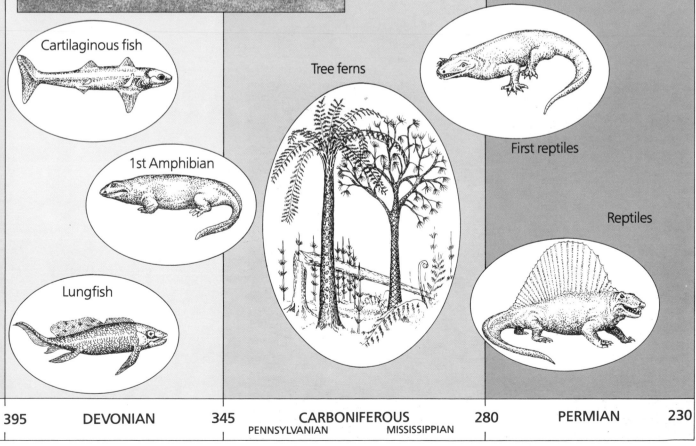

Cartilaginous fish

Tree ferns

First reptiles

1st Amphibian

Reptiles

Lungfish

| 395 | DEVONIAN | 345 | CARBONIFEROUS | 280 | PERMIAN | 230 |
| | | | PENNSYLVANIAN   MISSISSIPPIAN | | | |

Middle life

The word *Mesozoic* means 'middle life'. The Mesozoic era is divided into three periods: the Triassic, Jurassic and Cretaceous.

The Triassic period saw the development of reptiles, including long-necked Plesiosaurs, dolphin-like Ichthyosaurs and early turtles in the seas. By the end of the period the ancestors of the dinosaurs, pterosaurs (flying reptiles) and crocodiles were all established. Lucky fossil hunters occasionally find dinosaur fossils in late Triassic rocks, but much more common are ammonites which are collected by many enthusiasts. These molluscs, which had tentacles, lived in usually spiral-shaped shells divided into chambers. Ammonites lived throughout the Mesozoic era, but none of the many species lived very long. Hence, ammonites are valuable index fossils. For example, Jurassic rocks in Britain are divided into 74 zones, each of which is named after an ammonite species.

Jurassic rocks also contain other interesting fossils, including belemnites. Shaped like bullets, belemnites were once thought to be thunderbolts, hurled to earth by the Devil. In fact, they are the remains of cephalopods (molluscs similar to cuttlefish). On land, dinosaurs flourished and some reached enormous sizes. The Jurassic period also saw the appearance of the first known bird, the reptile-like *Archaeopteryx*.

The Cretaceous period saw the evolution of flowering plants. It was also the period when the best known of all dinosaurs, the ferocious *Tyrannosaurus*, wandered the earth. But at the end of the Cretaceous period the dinosaurs, which had

Right Dinosaurs, such as the carnivore *Tyrannosaurus rex* and the herbivore *Triceratops*, dominated the Mesozoic era.
Below This fossil ammonite came from Jurassic rocks.

dominated the earth for more than 100 million years, became extinct, along with the Plesiosaurs, Ichthyosaurs and the ammonites. The reason for the extinctions is still debated by geologists. One recent suggestion is that a massive meteorite struck our planet, raising a cloud of dust which blocked out sunlight and changed the earth's climate. The large reptiles could not survive the sudden drop in temperature, nor could many of the plants which they relied on for their food.

Right Fossil belemnites from the lower Jurassic period.

Recent life

The word *Cenozoic* means 'recent life'. The Cenozoic era is divided into two periods: the Tertiary and the Quaternary. These names are survivors of an old classification of rocks into four groups: Primary, Secondary, Tertiary and Quaternary. Geologists no longer use the terms Primary and Secondary, but they have retained Tertiary and Quaternary.

The start of the Tertiary period marked the beginning of a new phase in earth history, the fast increase in the variety of mammals and birds. Mammals had existed at least since the start of the Jurassic period, but it was only after the extinction of the dinosaurs that they made much evolutionary progress.

By the end of the Paleocene epoch, the first epoch in the Tertiary period, there were 28 orders of mammals. Development continued through the Eocene and Oligocene epochs, reaching a peak in the Miocene. One significant development was the increase in the size and complexity of the brains of many species, particularly the primates. In the Pliocene epoch, human-like apes had appeared. Many of their fossils have recently been unearthed, especially in East Africa.

In the Quaternary period, the Pleistocene epoch was marked by a great Ice Age. This consisted of glacial periods when the ice advanced and interglacial periods when it was warmer than it is today. Many animal species became extinct. However, human development continued, culminating in the emergence of modern people about 50,000 years ago.

Fossils of primates and early human-like species are rare. But fossil hunters can find a rich flora and fauna in Cenozoic rocks laid down on the sea-bed. Most species are similar to those living today. Common fossils include bivalves, crustacea, gastropods, bony fish and occasional sharks, especially their teeth.

The 8-metre high *Baluchitherium* was one of many now extinct mammals which lived in the Miocene epoch.

Above The complete bodies of extinct woolly mammoths from the late Pleistocene epoch have been found in the frozen subsoil of Siberia. This remarkable fossil mammoth, on display in a Leningrad museum in the USSR, died about 45,000 years ago.

Below left Louis Leakey, his wife Mary, and his son Richard, shown here, have made important discoveries of fossils of early human-like creatures in East Africa.

Below An artist's impression of hominids (human-like creatures) over the last four million years. The reconstructions are based on fossil evidence.

Australopithecus   *Homo erectus*   *Homo sapiens*
Homo habilis   *Neanderthal man*

Collecting rocks and minerals

Collecting rocks and minerals is a popular hobby. 'Rock hounds', as American enthusiasts are called, visit places where rocks are exposed, such as beaches, cliffs and road cuttings. They take with them a basic kit, which often includes a geological hammer, a chisel, a magnifying glass, a penknife and a geological map of the area.

Beginners often find it difficult to identify rocks and minerals. But most collectors soon learn the most common types. One way is to buy a cheap collection of specimens which can be carried around and compared with rocks in the field.

Experienced collectors use a series of tests to identify unknown minerals. One test is hardness. The hardness of minerals is graded on the Mohs' scale. On this scale, talc, the softest mineral, has a hardness of 1 and diamond a hardness of 10. Quartz has a hardness of 7. On beaches, people may mistake glass for quartz. But quartz scratches glass, while glass will not scratch quartz.

A few minerals, such as green malachite, are identifiable by their colour, but colour is often misleading. The streak (the powdered form of the

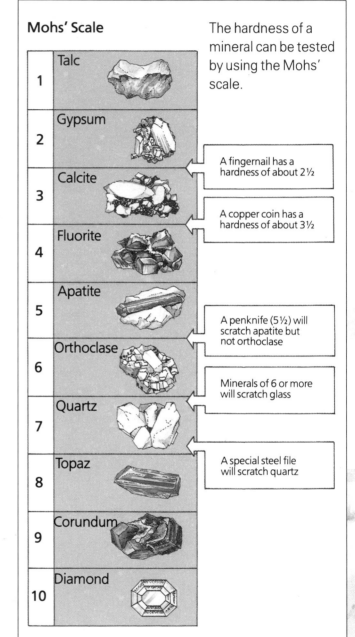

Mohs' Scale

The hardness of a mineral can be tested by using the Mohs' scale.

1	Talc
2	Gypsum
3	Calcite
4	Fluorite
5	Apatite
6	Orthoclase
7	Quartz
8	Topaz
9	Corundum
10	Diamond

A fingernail has a hardness of about 2½

A copper coin has a hardness of about 3½

A penknife (5½) will scratch apatite but not orthoclase

Minerals of 6 or more will scratch glass

A special steel file will scratch quartz

Collecting rocks and minerals is a fascinating hobby. Collectors use a basic kit to extract specimens. They record their finds in notebooks so that they can later label the specimens accurately.

mineral) is also helpful in some cases (see page 24). Books on minerals help by giving detailed descriptions. These may indicate whether a mineral is transparent or opaque, the specific gravity, which can be measured with simple scientific equipment, and cleavage. Cleavage is the way a mineral splits apart when struck.

All minerals have special crystal forms, though many crystals found in rocks are deformed and are not helpful in identification. Mineralogists also use simple chemical tests. For example, the powder of minerals containing copper burns blue or green in a flame, while minerals containing sodium turn the flame yellow. Some minerals, such as halite (rock salt), dissolve in water. Others dissolve in various acids. Other properties which are useful in identifying some minerals include magnetism, radioactivity and luminescence.

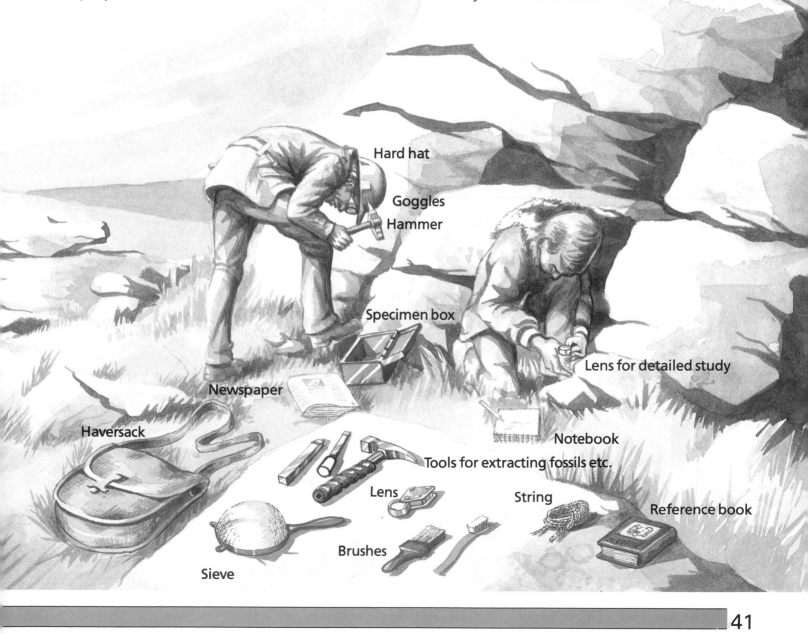

Hard hat

Goggles

Hammer

Specimen box

Newspaper

Lens for detailed study

Haversack

Notebook

Tools for extracting fossils etc.

Lens

String

Reference book

Brushes

Sieve

Collecting fossils

Fossil hunters are advised to spend time in a local museum, where specimens are displayed. Museum curators can often supply information about fossil sites, but remember that permission must be obtained to visit sites on private property. Also remember to observe safety rules, such as checking the times of tides. Avoid climbing cliffs. Instead, search among the broken rocks at the base of cliffs. In spring, in particular, many beaches are littered with fresh rocks which crashed down during winter storms.

Fossil hunters use the same tools as rock and mineral collectors. They also carry plenty of packing materials to protect fragile specimens. If you watch professional paleontologists at work, you will see that they take enormous care. Before removing, say, a fossil bone, they clean the surface and coat it with a protective plastic. Then they place wet paper on the fossil, followed by sacking dipped in plaster of Paris. When this coating hardens, they can safely lift the fossil. Amateurs who find interesting specimens, which are large and difficult to remove, should seek the help of professional paleontologists.

Books on fossils help collectors to identify specimens. Fossil collections in museums are also helpful. Museum curators will often offer advice. At home, fossils must be cleaned. Some collectors remove the rock around fossils with electrical tools. Acids can be used, but must be handled with care. Some fossils, such as those made of pyrite, slowly disintegrate in the air. To preserve them, they should be coated with a special cellulose solution.

Below Valuable dinosaur bones are carefully protected with plastics, wet paper and plaster before they are removed. In this way, they can be lifted in one piece.

Each specimen in a collection should be labelled, not only with the specimen's name, but also the rock formation and the site where it was found. The more information that accompanies a collection, the more valuable it becomes.

Above At the Dinosaur National Museum, in Utah and Colorado in the USA, geologists have uncovered large numbers of fossils of dinosaurs and other creatures. The fossils have been exposed on the sides of steep valleys worn by rivers.

Glossary

Amphibian   An animal adapted for life in water and on land.

Arthropods   A large group of animals with segmented bodies and jointed legs. They include Arachnids, crustacea and insects.

Atmosphere   The layer of gases around the earth.

Birthstone   A gemstone associated with a month of the year.

Bivalves   Molluscs, such as oysters, with shells consisting of two parts, which are hinged together.

Cambrian   The first period of the Paleozoic era, named after *Cambria*, the Latin word for Wales.

Carboniferous   A period in the Paleozoic era, named after the coal (carbon) beds formed at that time.

Cartilaginous fish   Fish, such as sharks, with skeletons of cartilage (gristle) instead of bone.

Cretaceous   A period in the Mesozoic era, named after *creta*, the Latin word for chalk.

Crustacea   A large group of Arthropods, including crabs, lobsters, shrimps, sand-hoppers and woodlice.

Crystal   A solid that has a geometric shape because the atoms of a mineral are arranged in a regular pattern.

Devonian   A period in the Paleozoic era, named after the county of Devon in southwestern England.

Dinosaurs   Extinct reptiles which lived during the Mesozoic era.

Fossil fuels   The fuels coal, oil and natural gas, all of which were formed from the remains of once-living organisms.

Gastropods   A group of molluscs, including limpets, slugs and snails.

Geologists   Scientists who study the earth, its composition, structure and history.

Ice Ages   Ages in earth history when ice spread over regions which now have warm or mild climates.

Jurassic   A period in the Mesozoic era, named after the Jura Mountains in France.

Magma   Hot liquid rock below the earth's surface, containing dissolved gases.

Mammoth   An extinct species of elephant.

Meteorite   A meteor (a lump of rock or metal) which strikes the earth's surface.

Mohs scale   A scale range from 1 to 10 for measuring the hardness of minerals. It is named after Friedrich Mohs, an Austrian mineralogist who devised it in 1822.

Molluscs   A large group of soft-bodied animals, most of which have hard shells.

Ordovician   A period in the Paleozoic era, named after the Ordovices, an ancient tribe who once lived in that part of North Wales, where Ordovician rocks were studied.

Paleontologists   Scientists who study fossils.

Permian   A period in the Paleozoic era, named after the Perm district in the USSR.

Petrified   Turned to stone.

Precipitation   The separation of a solid from a liquid by chemical action.

Primates   A group of mammals which includes human beings and animals that resemble them.

Resin   The sap of a tree which hardens to form amber.

Rock   A mass of hard mineral matter. Rocks need not be solid. Sand and mud are also rocks. Coal, a fossil fuel, is often called a rock, though most rocks are inorganic.

Silica   A chemical combination of the elements silicon and oxygen, called silicon dioxide.

Silurian   A period in the Paleozoic era, named after the Silures, an ancient tribe who lived in that part of Wales where Silurian rocks were first studied.

Solar system   The Sun and all the other bodies, including planets, moons, asteroids, comets and meteors, that rotate around it.

Stalactite   An icicle-like formation made of calcite hanging from the roof of a limestone cave.

Stalagmite   A column of calcite rising from the floor of a limestone cave.

Triassic   A period in the Mesozoic era, named after the fact that the strata of this period in Germany are divided into three main layers.

Trilobites   Extinct arthropods which lived on the sea-bed. Some of them may have resembled woodlice.

Water vapour   Invisible moisture in the atmosphere.

Further reading

Dineen, Jacqueline *Focus on Aluminium* (Wayland, 1988).

Halstead, L.B. *Hunting the Past* (Hamish Hamilton, 1982).

Lambert, David *The Cambridge Guide to Prehistoric Life* (Cambridge University Press, 1985).

Lambert, David *The Earth in Space* (Wayland, 1988).

Lambert, Mark *Focus on Copper* (Wayland, 1988).

Lambert, Mark *Focus on Oil* (Wayland, 1986).

Lambert, Mark *Fossils* (Kingfisher Books, 1984).

Lye, Keith *Focus on Gold* (Wayland, 1987).

Lye, Keith *Minerals and Rocks* (Kingfisher Books, 1986).

Major, Alan *Collecting Fossils* (Bartholomew, 1974).

Rickard, Graham *Focus on Diamonds* (Wayland, 1987).

Rickard, Graham *Focus on Silver* (Wayland, 1987).

Rowland-Entwistle, T. *Focus on Coal* (Wayland, 1987).

Stiegeler, Stella E. (editor) *A Dictionary of Earth Sciences* (Pan Books, 1978).

Picture acknowledgements

The publishers would like to thank the following for allowing their photographs to be reproduced in this book: Bruce Coleman Ltd 10 (Owen Drayton), 24 (right/Jane Burton), 25 (bottom/Steve Kaufman), 29 (Michael Fogden), 31, 37 (Jane Burton), 39 (top/R.I.M. Campbell), 43 (David Robinson); Geoscience Features Library 6, 11, 12, 13 (top), 15 (top), 15 (bottom left), 15 (bottom right), 16, 23 (top), 23 (bottom), 24 (left), 25 (top right), 35, 36, 42, front cover (main picture), front cover (inset), back cover; Hutchison Library 27 (bottom); Keith Lye 14; Novosti Press Agency 39 (bottom); Christine Osborne 7 (top), 19 (top); Oxford Scientific Films 13 (bottom/Breck P. Kent), 17 (bottom/Breck P. Kent), 20 (Michael Fogden), 22, 26 (Breck P. Kent), 28 (Kjell Sandved), 33 (David Wrigglesworth); Planet Earth Pictures 9 (M. Stroud); TOPHAM 7; ZEFA 17 (top), 18 (both), 19 (bottom), 21 (both), 27 (top). All illustrations by Malcolm Walker.

Index